M000012620

It's Fun To Be A
Grandma

BECKY FREEMAN JOHNSON

HARVEST HOUSE PUBLISHERS

EUGENE, OREGON

Unless otherwise indicated, all Scripture quotations are taken from the HOLY BIBLE, NEW INTERNATIONAL VERSION®. NIV®. Copyright©1973, 1978, 1984 by the International Bible Society. Used by permission of Zondervan. All rights reserved.

Verses marked TLB are taken from *The Living Bible,* Copyright ©1971. Used by permission of Tyndale House Publishers, Inc., Wheaton, IL 60189 USA. All rights reserved.

Verses marked KJV are taken from the King James Version of the Bible.

Verses marked NKJV are taken from the New King James Version. Copyright ©1982 by Thomas Nelson, Inc. Used by permission. All rights reserved.

Verses marked (NIrV®) are taken from the HOLY BIBLE, NEW INTERNATIONAL READER'S VERSION®. NIrV®. Copyright © 1995, 1996, 1998 by International Bible Society®. Used by permission. All rights reserved worldwide.

Harvest House Publishers has made every effort to trace the ownership of all quotes. In the event of a question arising from the use of a quote, we regret any error made and will be pleased to make the necessary correction in future editions of this book.

Becky Freeman Johnson: Published in association with the literary agency of WordServe Literary Group, Ltd., 10152 S. Knoll Circle, Highlands Ranch, CO 80130

Cover by Jeff Franke Design and Illustration, Minneapolis Minnesota

Cover photo © Nick White / Digital Vision / Getty Images

IT'S FUN TO BE A GRANDMA

Copyright © 2007 by Becky Freeman Johnson
Published by Harvest House Publishers
Eugene, Oregon 97402

Library of Congress Cataloging-in-Publication Data
Johnson, Becky Freeman, 1959-
  It's fun to be a grandma / Becky Freeman Johnson.
      p. cm. (HeartLite stories)
  ISBN-13: 978-0-7369-1807-7
  ISBN-10: 0-7369-1807-8
  1. Grandmothers—Religious life. I. Title.
BV4528.5.J64 2007
242'.6431—dc22
                                    2006016226

All rights reserved. No part of this publication may be reproduced, stored in a retrieval system, or transmitted in any form or by any means—electronic, mechanical, digital, photocopy, recording, or any other—except for brief quotations in printed reviews, without the prior permission of the publisher.

Printed in China

07 08 09 10 11 12 13 14 / RDS-SK / 10 9 8 7 6 5 4 3 2 1

□ □ □

To Ethan and Nate
and all my grandchildren to come!

□ □ □

Acknowledgments

Thank you to two grandmothers who gave me some wonderful material for this book just by being you. First my own huggable, storybook grandmother, Nonnie. Then, my mother, Ruthie, who is the world's best "Granny" to my children, along with my nieces and nephews.

In addition, I wrote this little book with a heart full of love for Ethan and Nate and all my future grandchildren to come. I'm at that wonderful stage of life where grandbabies are just coming into the world, and hopefully many more will follow in the years ahead. As friend and editor Rebecca Currington described it, "You've simply not been born until you've held your first grandchild!"

My heartfelt gratitude to the folks at Harvest House Publishers, particularly Bob Hawkins, Jr., Terry Glaspey, Carolyn McCready, and LaRae Weikert for not just talking about grace but for actually being "God's love with skin on" to me when my life as I knew it blew into so many pain-filled pieces. Thank you from the depths of my soul for reminding me of who I am and trusting me to continue sharing my heart through the written word.

Thanks to the ever-encouraging and talented Jean Christen and Barbara Gordon for doing the fine-tuning on this manuscript.

Last, but certainly not least, I want to thank the love of my life, my husband, Greg Johnson, for putting me back together again and for loving me truly, deeply, and madly every blessed day of my life. Your kind and tender husbanding has created the garden from which I've been able to blossom into an ecstatically happy wife, serene mother, more creative writer, and now, euphoric grandmother. Oh, and you just happen to be the world's best literary agent. I love you so!

Contents

1

My Hero

If it was going to be easy, it never would have started with something called "labor."

AUTHOR UNKNOWN

had been in labor for 27 hours, and now the hardest part of all was here. Transition. The stage where you dare your husband to even THINK about having sex with you again. This was a home birth, my first baby, and in between the agony of pushing, I lay back on the bed. Too far into the process to get to the hospital and beg for drugs, I prayed for an out-of-body experience. In spite of the midwife's encouragement, in spite of my husband's efforts to soothe me, I wanted to quit. Take my toys and go home. But I *was* home, and the only toy I had brought along with me was coming down the birth canal at the speed of a sloth.

"Can't you just push the baby back up and let me stay pregnant for the rest of my life?" I asked the mid-wife during one brief respite. "Really, I've decided I don't mind...just get me OUTTA THIS PAIN!"

Just then, rounding the corner, was the face of my mother. *Yes,* I thought, *I want my Mommy.* I had no idea she'd just risen from her knees in the bedroom next door, praying for me, for God's mercy, for my safety and that of her first grandchild's. Having lost her first baby due to toxemia at full term in a modern hospital 24 years earlier, fear was gripping her heart. Now calmed by the balm of the Holy Spirit, she had risen to tend to her daughter's pain.

"Becky," she said, looking me full in the face. "Listen to me, Darling. *You are my hero!* You can do this."

A hero? I was my mother's hero? Well, then...OKAY. ALL-RIGHTY. Maybe I could do this after all. Mother said I could, and she was rarely wrong. Besides how could a hero not complete her mission? With all the strength left in me, I pushed again.

"Oh, Becky!" Mother exclaimed from her vantage point at the end of the bed behind the midwife. "I see the baby's head. He has dark hair!"

I think it was the first time I fully realized there was an actual living person inside me. Buoyed by the thought that this labor really might have an ending, and that the ending might bring a real baby to my arms, I pushed again. And again. And again.

"He's here!" my mother exclaimed. "He's here and he's beautiful. A boy! Oh, Becky, Becky. You DID it, Darlin'..."

Within seconds a heavy, warm lump of writhing miracle lay on my tummy and breasts. The sun rose; angels sang. I was a mother! And my own mother was no longer just a wife and mom. In that instant she became Granny.

All the next day, she later told me, she stopped strangers in stores and paused to chat with clerks she didn't know to tell them, to impress them with the fact that there was a new life, a darling baby boy who had arrived in our world and had sprinkled us all with fairy baby dust. She was as high as a kite, drunk on the joy of new grandmotherhood. Nobody loves newborn babies like my mother; no one speaks "baby talk" as fluently. With the arrival of her own personal grandchild, she had truly come into her prime.

Now, seven grandchildren later, my mother has seen me through many life transitions that were not of my own choosing. Each time I called her or cried in her arms saying, "Mother, I cannot survive this," she would gather strength from her private prayer time and come back to me with the message I needed to hear to keep going: "Becky, you are my hero. You can do this."

And sure enough, I found I could continue on through the labors and heartaches and questions of life. Because, eventually, at the end of the pain and the end of the work, I knew the sun would rise and with it, bring a newborn miracle to my soul.

I learned this from my friend, my comforter, my faithful labor coach—*my* hero: my mother.

☐ ☐ ☐

A woman giving birth to a child has pain because her time has come; but when her baby is born she forgets the anguish because of her joy that a child is born into the world.

John 16:21

2

The Keeper of Stories

_The richer a family is in stories, the
greater the legacy to pass on._

PETER STILLMAN, _FAMILIES WRITING_

My Aunt Etta, the oldest female of seven children, was the first writer in our family. Once she met with publishing success, she encouraged her little sister, my mother—the only other girl in the family—to write professionally. Within a couple of decades my mother, in turn, introduced me to the ecstasy of writing and the agony of rejection letters. In time, Mom and I wrote two books together: _Worms in My Tea_ and _Help! I'm Turning into My Mother._ Passing on the family writing torch, my mom and I became my little sister's number one fans the first time we read Rachel's quirky prose and laughed aloud. Yesterday I got an e-mail from my mother that caused me to squeal aloud.

"Becky, your sister and her babies are gathered around my kitchen table and the only thing missing is you. Rachel just got a call from her agent, and a publisher has bid on her first book. Celebrate with us! And by the way, Tori, at a precocious two-and-one-half years, is trying to type on my keyboard, sounding out letters as she goes. Perhaps she'll be the next female writer to bloom on our family writing tree."

The joy of words well-spoken and well-written was as much a part of my upbringing as warm cookies and cold milk after school. Why? Because words were the tools used to help us taste life twice. An experience, be it funny or poignant, was immediately ground into the wheat of words for story bread and shared between the generations by phone, letters, and across kitchen tables.

My mother, a proud grandmother of seven, especially loves to retell the things that come out of the mouths of babes. I received an email last week from her that made me grin. My mom's granddaughter, Tori (who is also my beloved niece), is an amazing little conversationalist. Part of her charm is that she substitutes the letter "y" for more than a few consonants. So "You're welcome..." comes out "You yecome." And "Would you like lotion on your legs?" becomes "Would you yike yotion on you yegs?"

Mother wrote, "Tori walked into the kitchen yesterday with one of those big candy gummy lizards. Grasping the lizard's head with one hand and the tail with her other hand, she pulled and pulled. Then she looked up at me, her brown eyes enormous and said, 'Wow! That's a yong, yong, yizard!'"

I laughed aloud and knew this little anecdote would end up in a big, brown envelope labeled "Grandchildren's Cuties" to be recycled into stories that would be written, spoken, told, and retold to Tori as she grows from baby into young lady into adult. I know this because it is an unspoken understanding that in our family the females are the "Keepers of Stories."

One need not be a professional writer or speaker to be the family's Keeper of Stories. One only needs to be a grandmother, with her ears wide open, her heart full, and her pen and scratch paper ready. And who knows, those notes may someday end up in a published book, like this one, for other grandmothers to read and enjoy.

Even if it never makes the bestseller list, you'll have the joy of knowing you've given your grandchildren, budding forth from the family tree, the yong, yong, yegacy of laughter and love served up with the joy of words.

□ □ □

Thy mother is like a vine in thy blood, planted by the waters: she was fruitful and full of branches.

EZEKIEL 19:10 KJV

3

Frugality in a Flower-Print Apron

*I loved my grandparents' home. Everything
smelled older, worn but safe; the food
aroma had baked itself into the furniture.*

<small>SUSAN STRASBERG</small>

One of my warmest childhood memories centers around a little white house with blue shutters, a picket fence, and a line of deep pink crepe myrtle trees. Around that house in Sweetwater, Texas, dust and tumbleweeds blew relentlessly. Inside the house was my Nonnie. Think Mrs. Doubtfire, complete with the silver hair pulled up in a soft bun, the calico dress and apron, the sensible shoes, and the soothing presence and voice—and you have the picture of my grandmother.

My grandmother's kitchen was small but oh, the life that

bubbled inside! I preferred listening to the theatrical storytelling of my many aunts and cousins, along with my own Lucy Ricardo-like mother, than watching any play or movie. I can still smell the hot coffee brewing in the tall, electric chrome pot and see quiet Nonnie, ever-aproned and stirring a pot of black-eyed peas or peach cobbler makings on the old gas stove.

Nonnie's brown arms were always tanned from the sunny hours she spent tending her flower bed. And if I were very lucky, while gardening she'd catch a baby horned toad to the delight of us grandkids. I spent hours making mud pies, collecting rocks, and playing "mama" to the cute baby horned toads—creating little houses for them out of cardboard boxes and colorful quilting scraps.

And how well I remember the comforting feeling of being cushioned against Nonnie's grandmotherly bosom, perfect twin pillows for a drowsy grandchild.

Nonnie never had much money, but she was rich in family. One day I asked my Aunt Etta about her memories of Nonnie, and it was Nonnie's frugality that first sprang to my aunt's sharp mind.

"Nonnie and I lived through the Great Depression surrounded by men—my father and five brothers. I was the only girl until my little sister, Ruthie, was born, the year I turned 13. It was expected that the oldest daughter would don an apron and help Nonnie in the kitchen, so of course I did. A meal for eight always presented a major problem since everyone in our small town was poor, and my father adamantly refused to 'go on relief.'"

"What did you eat with so many mouths and so little money?" I asked.

"Nonnie would make a breakfast for eight out of cornmeal poured into boiling water—mush. Mush was good with syrup...

if you had any. If not, you stirred sugar into it, and if you were lucky enough to have spices, cinnamon. I watched her save any leftover mush to fry for the evening meal."

She must have noted my raised eyebrows, for she continued, knowing she had my attention, "She made gravy by beating lard, adding flour, and instead of milk, which we rarely had, she used water. Then she made water biscuits with lard, water, flour, salt, and a wee bit of sugar. I never saw her throw one biscuit away. 'They'll be good split and toasted in the oven tonight,' she'd remind us."

I laughed, as it was something so typical of Nonnie.

Aunt Etta continued, "I remember a perfect Thanksgiving dinner, years later, probably when you were about four or five years old, Becky. There was a huge turkey, browned and succulent. Dressing that melted in your mouth. Cranberry sauce, fruit salad, and desserts that were so rich they were almost immoral. I thought of those spartan days during the Depression and thanked the good Lord that our mother no longer was forced to scrimp, to make water gravy and mush."

Etta paused for a moment and smiled, remembering. "I carried dishes to the kitchen and noticed a spot on the floor. Bending over it, I examined it closely. Dressing? Someone had dropped it and someone else had stepped in it. Disgusting! 'What on earth is this?' I asked. Your Nonnie was close behind me. She leaned over my shoulder and said, 'Whatever it is, save it.'"

Though my grandmother and her children lived through poverty our generation may never understand, they learned that life is rich in so many other ways. A family can live a good while on cornmeal, biscuits, and gravy, though they may tire of the simple fare. Still, as long as there is the syrup of love and cinnamon of laughter in the heart of the family matriarch, hard times are not only survivable, they are thrivable.

□ □ □

Better a little with the fear of the LORD
than great wealth with turmoil. Better
a meal of vegetables where there is
love than a fatted calf with hatred.

PROVERBS 15:16-17

4

In Search of Grandma's Garden

---

*In the midst of winter, I found there was
within me an invincible summer.*

Albert Camus

I went to visit the home of my beloved assistant, Rose Dodson. It was a lovely spring morning, and we decided to have our coffee-cup conversation down in the trees near her garden.

"I call this my heirloom garden," Rose said, her long, golden curls bobbing behind her as she walked, "in memory of my grandmother's garden." Rose, with her delicate features and porcelain skin, and her love of long, flowing skirts, always looked to me as if she'd just walked out of the cover of *Victoria* magazine—a living cameo.

As we visited, Rose talked of a painful childhood, of how

her mother and father divorced when she was small and that the solace she sought was found in her grandmother's arms. Later, as a young adult, when her husband left her for another woman three days after the birth of her first daughter, it was back to her grandmother's house she went, seeking love and the familiarity of her home and garden. I asked Rose if she would share her memories of this time with me, and one morning she handed me the following page from her journal.

The fresh dew glistening in the sunlight and the music of waking birds signaled that Grandma would not be sitting idly in the house. Oh no, not Grandma. On such a fine spring morning she would be found tending her garden or digging a new flower bed. Wasting such a morning would be close to sin as far as she was concerned. I was twenty, my life was in turmoil, and I hungered for a visit with Grandma, along with a plateful of speckled butter beans.

Sure enough, as I approached her small, white, frame house, I saw her kneeling, transplanting touch-me-nots along the fence line. When I was a little girl, Grandma had allowed me to pick the little popping seed pods from these flowers with the funny-sounding name. I remember carrying my treasure home in a small, brown, paper bag, feeling like Grandma's flower princess.

Watching Grandma work in her garden over the years was a pleasantly familiar scene. She always wore a big straw hat or sunbonnet to protect her fair skin from the harsh Louisiana sun and light cotton clothing to keep cool. Her hands were never without her flower-print gloves when she worked outside. She was a living portrait that appeared many times in my mind's eye, always soothing and cheering my heart.

As I watched Grandma rise from her beautiful bed of flowers, I knew she would have to retire from her beloved garden before long. Her movements were slow and pain-ridden, but she still greeted me with a generous smile and folded me inside her warm grandma hug. Little did I know at the time that Grandma would be making heaven her home within a few short months of this day, which would turn out to be our last visit together.

The smell of breakfast still lingered as we entered the immaculate little house with hardwood floors and Naugahyde furniture. Smoked bacon, homemade biscuits and gravy, eggs, and of course, the savory smell of chicory coffee tempted my senses. It had been a long time since I'd come to Grandma's house, but as far as I could tell, thankfully, not much had changed. The old clock on the television began to chime and, as it rang through the kitchen, sentiment almost got the best of me.

"Let's take a look at my garden," Grandma finally offered.

I thought she'd never ask.

Looking up from Rose's journalings, I was reminded of how it was the old, well-known familiarities we long for and pilgrimage to in times of change and crisis. The chime of an old clock sitting on the black-and-white television, the smell of chicory coffee, the sight of familiar vines winding their way up decades-old poles, Grandma's hug. These things together make up the haven of hope that welcomes grandchildren of all ages and stages when the world grows cold and lonely and unfamiliar. With a grandmother's prayers and love, grandchildren discover their own internal gardens of continual hope.

The LORD will guide you continually...
you shall be like a watered garden.

ISAIAH 58:11 NKJV

5

A Grandma's Courage

Often the test of courage is not to die but to live.
Vittorio Alfieri

In Bernie Bland's 50-plus-year marriage to Bob Bland, plumber-turned-pastor-turned-visionary/missionary, this curly haired grandmother has experienced more excitement than most of us could amass in two lifetimes. As cofounder of Teen Missions International (TMI) she almost died from malaria; she was knocked unconscious in the jungles of Peru by an absentminded, oar-wielding teenager; and she has had her body invaded by a myriad of amoebas from foreign lands. She's cooked innumerable meals in gargantuan quantities over primitive fire pits, washed truckloads of used clothing to send to poverty-stricken children, and has comforted and encouraged thousands of teenagers far from home—and all without complaint. When I was 15, Bob and Bernie were the teen leaders for the mission trip I took to help build an orphanage. They worked alongside us mixing mortar, laying brick, and digging ditches in El Salvador and Guatemala.

To my way of thinking, Bernie should be found next to the word "trouper" in Webster's. Coleading an organization that has sent more than 34,000 Americans (and just as many third-world national teens) to serve in various parts of the world would leave most of us dreaming of retirement. But retirement has never been in the Blands' long-range plans.

In late 1997 I went to visit her after she had foot surgery. Our visit took place at the primitive TMI Boot Camp filled with teens preparing to embark on their adventure. Bernie looked up at me from her bed with those ever-young eyes, now edged with sorrow, and said, "Oh, Honey, it's been a terrible year."

"I know," I offered as I moved to her side, blinking back tears. "I know."

I knew and yet I do not know. How could I know what it was like to fall in love with an ebony-haired grandbaby named Joel with eyes the color of rich mahogany and a smile as big as Christmas morning? I'd never been a grandmother. How could I know how it felt to watch this adorable boy grow to a young man so handsome and charming he magnetized rooms full of people with his presence.

How could I possibly fathom what it was like to walk into a hospital emergency room and see this same grandson—captain of the football team—lying paralyzed from the neck down, a casualty of an impetuous dive into a too-shallow pool?

I tried to imagine Bernie holding hands with her family as they encircled Joel, this man-child, this joy of their family. How must she have felt as she stood powerless to help, except to offer prayers and her presence, as they waited out the agonizing hours before Joel's spirit slipped from the earth to heaven's unseen welcome? Observing a family's grief and actually facing the truth that someone beloved has vanished from our daily lives are continents of experience apart, separated by a sea of pain.

I sensed this might be the blow that would send Bernie into retirement. I was wrong. The Bland motto is "When the going gets tough, the tough get going." When I asked Bernie where she most liked to travel, she named the most primitive places on earth.

"Why?" I asked.

"Because I love a challenge," she replied unflinchingly.

There are too many precious children in want of the Savior's love—from AIDS orphans in Africa to adorable toddlers and teenagers with big hopes, huge questions, and no experience. Too many needs to linger long at the well of tears. So while grief grips the Bland family, life will go forward. Love still goes on. Bernie will venture out to plan a camp-wide meal or mend a homesick teenager's heart. The hope of the future—clad in dirty overalls and muddy boots—awaits them.

Today, there is an orphanage founded by Teen Missions that stands as a beacon of love to the AIDS-infected street orphans of Africa. It is called the House of Joel.

And I am convinced that a handsome hunk of a grandson, dark eyes glistening with eternal joy, is cheering the people on from heaven's sidelines...with a smile as big as Christmas morning.

*Even though I walk through the valley
of the shadow of death, I will fear
no evil, for you are with me; your rod
and your staff, they comfort me.*

PSALM 23:4

6

Sandwich-to-Go

Growing old ain't for sissies.
BETTE DAVIS

The sad day dawned when it became apparent that our beloved Nonnie had aged to the point that she could no longer live in her home out in West Texas without a relative in her small town to look after her. Longtime friends and a paid attendant had done the best they could, but Nonnie was losing her hold on reality. She insisted on getting up every 30 to 45 minutes at night to make her way to the bathroom, and at least once a night she fell and bruised or cut herself in new places. Mother and her five siblings concurred: Nonnie would move in with Mom. That was the way Mother wanted it.

One morning a few weeks after the move, it dawned on me that I had not been seeing much of my mother of late. I knew she was looking after Nonnie, but still, it was only an hour-and-a-half drive to my house. I decided to give her a call.

"I miss you too," she assured me. "But last night was the twenty-fourth night I have slept in the twin bed beside Nonnie, getting up with her five and six times a night to make sure she doesn't fall when she gets up to go to the bathroom."

"Congratulations!" I commiserated. "Sounds like you've become a card-carrying member of the Sandwich Generation."

Many of you reading this book are sandwiched, tending to young grandchildren one day, helping an elderly parent the next. Caught in the middle, it can be difficult, and the burden may seem too heavy at times.

My mother continued the sandwich discussion. "Yes, but I don't think I'm a hero sandwich. I'm feeling more like a wilted lettuce on rye. You're not going to believe what happened," Mother said on the other end of the wire, but she was laughing, so it was a good sign. "We called your Uncle Lloyd, the doctor, and told him I hadn't had a full night's sleep in over three weeks, and it had been longer than that for Nonnie."

"Well," he said in his best doctor tone, "I'll fix that!" So at bedtime he brought out a sleeping pill—a huge, bright-red gel cap that looked like it could put a horse to bed for a month. She swallowed it down like a good girl, and we sat for a minute or two at the table saying goodnight to Lloyd, and then I took her into the bathroom to get her ready for bed. I helped her undress. I cleaned her bridge work while she brushed what was left of her own teeth.

"She bent over the sink, and the first thing I knew, she started to sway. I grabbed her and started leading her out of the bathroom, hoping I could get her to the bed before she went sound asleep. I could tell within a few steps we weren't going to make it. By the time I yelled for Uncle Lloyd and we struggled with her to the nearest chair, we were sweating profusely and she was snoring soundly!

"There's this about it," I told Lloyd as we huffed and puffed and got her into bed, "this is one night it looks like I'm going to get some rest!

"Little did I know! At two o'clock Nonnie rose off her pillow like some filmy apparition, determined to get up and go to the bathroom. She was just groggy enough to be really unsteady on her feet, so I had to yell for Uncle Lloyd to help me take her. We managed to get her back to bed, and she did go back to sleep without getting up again. But by seven the next morning, she was wider awake than I was!"

Even though she was exhausted, Mother sewed dresses for Nonnie—pretty pastel creations that were easy to get into. Both her daughters and daughters-in-law combed her lovely silver hair into a most becoming French twist. She spent her days quietly sitting in the living room rocker, her hands folded in her lap, her soft blue eyes gazing into the past. Every now and then she would give herself a mental health checkup.

"Cantaloupe," she would say quietly. "C-a-n-t-a-l-o-u-p-e." Then she would look at Mother and give her a beaming look of triumph, as if to say, "If I can still spell cantaloupe, I must be okay!"

One has to laugh when you can during the years of caring for aging and elderly parents or the stress would be overwhelming.

Perhaps you need someone to comfort you today. You might as well let it be me. There now, sit down. Put your feet up. Listen to me. You have to take time to "nurture the nurturer" of the family. So between changing diapers (or Depends), baby bottles (or cans of Ensure), plan a whole day off where you do nothing but pamper your own sweet self. Get a massage, go to a chick flick, take a guilt-free nap. Take good care of yourself, dear woman, and let the sunshine in.

After all, if Grandma ain't happy, ain't nobody happy.

☐ ☐ ☐

He who refreshes others will
himself be refreshed.

Proverbs 11:25

7

Nonnie's Eyes

Life is very rarely all ease or all struggles, and pity the human being who, in either condition, cannot find plenty to laugh about.

RUTHIE ARNOLD, MY MOM

I had my own wonderful memories of my grandmother Nonnie, the quintessential grandmother complete with a big bosom, flower-print dress, apron, and twinkling blue eyes. I was always curious, however, about the memories my own mother had of growing up in poverty with Nonnie as her mother. How was it in that old and creaky house on the corner of Broadway Street in the small West Texas town of Sweetwater?

As a child of the seventies, I grew up in a typical Wonder Years neighborhood, in a three-bedroom brick ranch in the suburbs, with Coppertone appliances in the kitchen and an olive green Country Squire station wagon parked in the driveway. My mother didn't have to work; Daddy's paycheck was modest but covered everything our family needed to enjoy roast beef on Sundays and beautiful fabrics for the colorful dresses Mother happily sewed for my sister and me. But I often pried my mother for memories of her childhood and of Nonnie, and my mother (storyteller that she is) was always happy to oblige. Since mother's father was alcoholic, depressed, and cranky, sweet-tempered Nonnie was the brightest spot in my mother's childhood.

"Sometimes Daddy would actually work," Mother told me one afternoon as we visited in our backyard porch swing behind the three bedroom ranch in suburbia. "This was great cause for celebration! But most of his time he spent closed away from the family in his bedroom, reading or sleeping. With Mother we would have our meals gathered around the old wooden table, talking and laughing and having a marvelous time. By this time we were all contributing money for groceries so the food was wonderful: Mother's fried chicken and steak, heaping bowls of mashed potatoes and cream gravy, nanner puddin'..."

"Mmmm," I said, having my own love affair with Nonnie's famous banana pudding. "Tell me a story about growing up in Nonnie's house."

"Well, let's see," Mother said. "I remember the antics of five big brothers playing tricks on each other and how much fun it was to watch them. But suddenly, it seemed, they all grew up at once and I was alone. I missed them, but I loved having Nonnie all to myself!"

I nodded. Mother continued, "When my handsome big brother James came home from Korea, he started dating my best friend, Martha. Not only that, but James had a car! He would often pick me up at noon for lunch, and Martha came along too. There's nothing more fun than having your big brother date your best friend."

"And did Nonnie like Martha?" I asked.

"Honey, Martha was like one of the family by this point. I will always remember the day Martha and I reached across Nonnie's table at the same time for the same fried chicken breast. We each connected with the chicken, and our eyes locked across the table, each grinning a wicked grin. I pulled; she pulled. James started to chuckle, and Nonnie began to laugh and sputter at the same time. 'Now girls...' she said.

"Martha was taller than I was, so I stood up to get a little more traction under my feet, keeping a firm grip on the chicken. I pulled again, but no luck. Martha rose to her feet, and laughing, we began to maneuver around the table, the chicken between us."

I laughed aloud at the scene in my mind. Mother laughed too, before continuing.

"By this time, James and Mother were trying to avoid getting grease and gravy all over them, since once Martha and I reached the front hallway, we had grease up to our elbows. The problem now became holding onto the slick chicken while not losing our strength—as we were almost too tickled to stand. As I recall, we resolved the issue by sitting down on the floor together, each still firmly gripping the chicken breast, and taking turns with bites."

"What did Nonnie do?" I asked.

"She just laughed and laughed, wiping her eyes on her apron and shaking her head. I knew it was an outrageous antic, and somewhere inside I remember thinking, 'What mother in the world would not only allow this, but enjoy it?'"

I looked up at my own mother, whose figure was trim and

her hair dyed a honey-red. I often thought how much she looked and acted like Lucy Ricardo. She was as funny and fun as she was beautiful. Though my mother's eyes are brown and not Nonnie's shade of blue, as she ages into the grandmother of my four children, I see more of Nonnie in them every day. She has Nonnie's twinkle and the same crinkles at the corners, welcoming joy into everyday moments.

I look in the mirror, now and again, and look for glimpses of Nonnie in me. And you know what? When I smile, I do believe I see her there.

□ □ □

A happy heart makes the face cheerful.

PROVERBS 15:13

8

Life Begins at 80!

She was the grandmother with the dancing eyes who loved to roller-skate with me, even into her late eighties, who baked exquisite little cookies, and spoke to the children in the town where she lived as though they were grown up and understood her.

DANIELLE STEELE

first met Vivian, an 87-years-young grandmother, at a speaking engagement. Even as I told stories from the platform I felt drawn to her eyes. They were like the eyes of a five-year-old child—filled with wonder and mischief. She reminded me of a small scarlet bird; on her tiny frame she wore a bright-red dress draped with a classic white shawl. Throughout my talk, Vivian maintained rapt eye contact, her white hair bobbing joyously as she laughed.

When I visited with her later in the church hallway, she exclaimed, "Listen, Honey—life begins at 80!"

Thus began a friendship that gave me a vision of the way I wanted to age, the sort of grandmother I hoped to be as the years went by.

Vivian had experienced major life changes in the last few years, changes that would have torpedoed a less unsinkable sort. She lost her beloved husband of 50-plus years and had moved several states away to relocate to a new home, where she lived alone, near her son's family. Rather than wait for others to reach out to her and welcome her to the neighborhood, Vivian dove in to community life right away and with vigor. In describing her transition time, Vivian giggled and said, "My kids thought I might be bored and lonely!"

Vivian obviously doesn't do bored, and she cannot stop accumulating friends long enough to be lonely. She told the preacher on her first Sunday at church that she wanted to start a club for anyone who is lonely. So weekly, women come walking, alone or with canes, and many are wheeled (from the local nursing home) to Vivian's living room to participate in her Let's Be Friends Club. There is no gossip allowed and no whining. Everyone is to bring something inspirational and uplifting to share. There are no refreshments except water. ("If I start serving punch, the next thing you know," says Vivian wisely, "they'll want cookies and then cake. You can't let refreshments get out of hand.")

The group has two official mottos: "I don't remember" and "I forgot."

Vivian's volunteer efforts amaze me. She worked with latchkey children after school for many months. She now volunteers by sorting clothes to sell at a local charity thrift shop called God's

Open Hands. When she announced to me that Meals on Wheels would happen the next day, I said, "Well, Vivian, that is wonderful. You deserve to have someone bring you a hot lunch."

She looked at me as though I'd just grown a tulip out of the top of my head. "Becky," she explained with patience, "I drive for the *elderly.*" It never crossed Vivian's mind that in her late eighties some might consider her a little on the elderly side.

In her seventies, Vivian decided to learn a foreign language, and she now speaks and reads Spanish beautifully. She has no time for fluffy reading, reading for pure entertainment. She reads only material that will inspire her or stretch her curious mind.

When Vivian broke her arm, she picked out a hot-pink cast. I have a favorite picture of her in a purple wet suit, riding a jet ski, her blue eyes twinkling. Life for Vivian is lived full-tilt and in vivid color.

On her ninetieth birthday I received a phone call saying, "Becky, I just called to tell you I'm still going strong. I got 90 birthday presents for my ninetieth birthday, and I just got off the back of a Harley."

Anytime I am tempted to complain about aging or achy bones, or feel sorry for myself, or seem a little lonely or forlorn—I remember this feisty friend of mine and know that life, most often, is what you are willing to dare, willing to give, willing to try. And it helps if you do it all with a childlike twinkle in your eye.

A few years ago, after meeting Vivian and also pondering what Jesus meant by telling us we had to be more like children to really understand His kingdom, I wrote this little poem and set it to a simple melody. (Stay tuned for my one-day-to-be-released CD: Ditties to Embarrass Your Children By.)

Growing Up to Be a Child

Mud-puddle miracles
Doodle-bug designs
Bursts of fun with bubblegum
Oh, to see life as a child!

"I love yous" big as rainbows
"I'm sorrys" from the heart
A kiss goodnight, a bear hug tight
To love as would a child!

"Let the children come to Me,"
Christ said with arms flung wide
Don't stop me now—
I'm coming, too
For I'm a child inside

I want to laugh from the belly
Risk playing a clown—
I'm giving up on growing old
Think I'll just start growing
D
O
W
N

□ □ □

*I tell you the truth, anyone who will
not receive the kingdom of God like
a little child will never enter it.*

Luke 18:17

9

Scrambled Legs

Oh, how I miss my mind.
BUMPER STICKER

When Nonnie suffered a stroke at age 85, Mother flew down to be with her in the hospital and called regularly to give me reports.

"She has no physical paralysis, but her mind is thoroughly scrambled. She's as giddy as a schoolgirl! Wouldn't that mortify her if she knew? She's still able to pop out of the bed, but she's not able to stay on her feet for sure or to know where she's going once she's on her feet. So I'm staying with her day and night here in the hospital."

"Are you getting any rest?" I asked.

"Enough. I have a cot by her bed, but she doesn't sleep much and doesn't like for me to. Last night when I tried to sleep, she gathered up her sheet and formed a long piece of it. Then she drew back like a teenage boy in a locker room and tried to pop me with it to wake me up!" The mental picture of my genteel little Nonnie trying to towel pop my mother was so incredible we both had to laugh. In times like these, you take humor where you can get it. A few days later Mother called me, chuckling again.

"Yesterday a physical therapist came in to see Nonnie. I'm sure he wanted to see if she'd suffered any muscular damage from the stroke. Wouldn't you know he'd be tall, dark, and handsome! The minute he walked in the door, Nonnie looked up and said, 'Bob Wheeler!'

"I knew she had mistaken him for her young preacher from back home and thought he had come all that way to see her. Talk about thrilled! Then he walked to her bed and took her hand, and she gazed up at him with pure rapture. Being a therapist, and not a preacher, the therapist began to gently move her arm up and down, which I'm sure she saw as just a sweet gesture as he talked with her about how she was feeling.

"All went well until he asked her, 'Mrs. Jones, do you mind if I look at your leg?' The expression on her face was so shocked. I was trying hard to keep from guffawing. Talk about disapproving! After a long minute, she looked up at him with a frown that would have frozen the Sahara.

"I guess not," she finally managed to say very coldly. "It'll hurt you worse'n it'll hurt me!"

I laughed out loud along with mother. She had discovered that even in the middle of the worst case scenarios there is humor to be found and shared.

Are you in a situation that seems to be humorless today? Look again. Put on what I call "Erma Bombeck" glasses and look at your circumstances as if they could be turned into a humor column or a sitcom tomorrow. In fact, you may want to write down what is happening as if it could be funny and practice the art of becoming a humorous person.

Humor won't make the hard times go away, but laughter is guaranteed to lighten your load during the moments you are chuckling. And sometimes a good laugh makes the difference between staying balanced and going over the edge.

I once read a statement by a Christian therapist that said, "Enter self-seriousness, exit humor. Exit humor, exit sanity." In other words, grandmas, if we don't laugh together, we are going to end up making pottery in an asylum together.

Laughter is vital for your spiritual, emotional, and mental health. So have at least one chuckle a day and you'll keep the little men with straightjackets away.

☐ ☐ ☐

A cheerful heart is good medicine.

PROVERBS 17:22

10

Little Boy Grandpa

*I myself have been flattered by the reputation
of never having quite grown up.*

WALT DISNEY

I heard a faint knock at my front door and moved to open it.
There stood Alex, age two, tow-headed with sky-blue eyes, smiling
and holding out a branch with some fuchsia berries adorning its
leaves.

"I found deese for you, Becky, way off down dere in da
woods," he lisped.

Out of the corner of my eye I saw Alex's grandpa—our
neighbor, Wally—standing off in the distance, beaming at his
beloved grandchild. My heart melted and I realized there was not
one child outside my door, but two. For little Alex and Grandpa
Wally are both kids, each in their own special way. Each lost in
the joy of wonder: Alex, of the branch; Wally, of his grandson.

⸢ // It's interesting the influence a grandchild has on a man—and how quickly small children can turn a large man into a boy again. // ⸤

Just a few days after the visit from Wally and little Alex, Wally's wife, Mary, went shopping and promised to be gone for the entire morning. Wally suddenly decided it would be a great idea, while the water was low, to dig some deep pools around the edges of the lake where we live. This, he reasoned, would create pools where fish could eventually congregate so fishermen could do the same. In truth, I strongly suspect Wally simply had a hankering to dig a big hole with a great big tractor.

"Hey, Jim Ed!" My eldest son, Zach, called to our next-door neighbor from our back porch, both of them having been beckoned outside by the sound of heavy machinery. (A Pied Piperesque call to every red-blooded man.) "What's goin' on down there?"

"Wally thinks he's going to dig himself a fishin' hole," Jim Ed replied, "I tried to tell him it was still too muddy."

"So what are you going to do now?" Zach asked.

"Well," drawled Jim Ed, "I think I'll sit right here and watch a tractor sink."

Sure enough, Jim Ed sat down just in time to see Wally drive the tractor six feet out from the edge of the pond and watch it sink nearly six feet under. Wally was in the mess up to his hip boots, and soon Zach, followed by his younger brother, Zeke, walked back into the house to give an updated blow-by-blow report.

"Mom," Zach informed me, "Wally's going to have to rent a big diesel truck to come pull that tractor out."

"Can you believe it?" Zeke echoed.

I could tell my teenaged sons were working hard at trying to disguise the little-boy excitement that kept threatening to creep into their manly, serious voices.

"Wonderful," I answered brightly. "Shall I make popcorn?"

"No time," Zach answered, no longer even attempting to hide his grin, "I gotta get back out there! Tell Dad and Gabe to come out here; they'll want to see this!"

That evening I visited with Wally's wife. She was sitting on the couch, staring numbly off into space, mumbling to herself. "Five hours. I only left him alone for five hours..."

After Wally read this story and admitted to finding it a mite funny, he wrote me the following note. "I just want to set the record straight, Becky. WE DID GET ONE FISHING HOLE! When that big diesel truck pulled out the tractor, it left a pretty nice bass hole. Not a big one, and we don't want to estimate dollars per cubic feet—but it will provide a home for several lake bass."

What can I say? Some grandpas will find any excuse to be little boys again.

God, save me. My troubles are like a flood.
I'm up to my neck in them. I'm sinking in deep
mud. I have no firm place to stand. I am out
in deep water. The waves roll over me.

PSALM 69:1-2 NIrV

11

Grandma Types

*Good news! The joy of grandparenting comes
when we can recognize our strengths and
limitations then learn to live within them.*

THE GRANDMOTHER BOOK

Betty Southard, Minister of Caring for the Hour of Power (Crystal Cathedral) and grandmother of eight, took time to listen to the hearts of grandmothers—all sorts of women in every conceivable grandparenting situation. The result of her listening and caring were poured into *The Grandmother Book,* coauthored with Jan Stoop. One of the fascinating discoveries in their research was that there are grandmother "types." Jan and Betty categorized them into four styles: The Doer Grandmother, The Dreamer Grandmother, The Discoverer Grandmother, and the Director Grandmother.

The Doer Grandmothers let no moss gather under their Nikes. They are "practical, down-to-earth, and realistic." They enjoy projects that can be completed quickly or anything that involves action—from picnics to hiking to swimming. This grandmother-on-the-go has an attention span that is fairly short, which is actually a bonus with small children because they both tire of an activity at about the same time. Another beauty of the doing grandma is that she has a "can do" attitude. Need something fixed? No problem! This grandma can do or find resources to help her get the task accomplished. My friend Georgia is a perfect example of the Doer Grandma, and I've often teased her about fidgeting when she gets bored. You can shock, exhaust, or tease Georgia, and she is unflappable. But bore her, and Honey, she's outta here.

Dreamer grandmothers are empathetic and intuitive, sensitive, and artistic. They love to read stories and rock babies, sing silly songs and cook creatively. They emphasize emotional and intellectual growth and want to see their grandchildren be all they can be. If you were to ask a grandchild to describe this grandmother in one word, that word would be "fun." My mother, Ruthie, was and is a dreamer. One minute she'd be absorbed in the joy of rocking a newborn, the next, entertaining a toddler with a funny face or silly song, and the next, asking an older grandchild what he really wanted to become and learn in this life. I imagine I'll be this sort of grandmother—unorganized, loose with directions, but creatively fun and sensitive.

Discoverer grandmothers are born teachers. They love projects like rock collections or butterflies hatching. They love to teach games and take children to plays, museums, and the zoo. My children's paternal grandmother, Beverly, is this grandma. With patience and determination she taught her grandchildren how to swim. And for each of the grandchildren who showed an artistic interest, she taught them how to paint with watercolors. Her gifts to the children were always interesting, creative, and educational. She loves to take the kids to museums and art shows. Beverly's children remember the day their ever-curious mother found a deceased frog and dissected it with them—never once thinking of it as gross or disgusting. This was pure science, a fascinating opportunity to teach a backyard biology lesson. She was, and is, a discoverer to the max!

Finally, there are director grandmothers. These are the women who have day planners and (to my everlasting shock) actually keep up with them. They have grandkids over for an afternoon and, instead of chaos reigning in the living room, these grandmas have them organized in productive activities like happy little worker bees. This is probably the grandma type I least identify with. I've left so many Day Planners at restaurants and other people's houses that it has become a standard "Becky joke" among friends and family. I once recommended a certain brand of planner/organizer notebook to a friend, and she quickly wrote the name down and quipped, "I just want to make sure I avoid buying this brand. Because, Becky, if this is what you are using to be an organized person, I hate to tell you this but let's face it: *It's not working.*"

What matters most, however, is not your type. God uses *every* brand of grandma to enrich the lives of grandchildren. The good news is God doesn't ask you to be a grandmother who does it all. He only asks you to be you, to bring your particular gifting to your grandchild's life. For He knew, from the beginning of time, just what your grandchildren would need in a grandmother.

And who would that be? Wonderfully, marvelously, fabulously, *uniquely* YOU.

□ □ □

Each one should test his own actions.
Then he can take pride in himself, without
comparing himself to somebody else.

GALATIANS 6:4

12

The World According to Grandbabies

If a child is to keep alive his inborn sense of wonder...he needs the companionship of at least one adult who can share it.

RACHEL CARSON

I've been collecting funny grandchildren stories off and on for several years now, and they never fail to make me chuckle, for some of the most hilarious dialogue comes between a grandmother and grandkids. Perhaps it is because, as one child wrote, "Grandmothers are the only people who have time to listen." What we grandmothers hear out of the mouths of babes is a goldmine of information (and comedy) in how the world works through the eyes and logic of a child.

Once my mother was driving with Gabe in the front seat. He was about three years old at the time (the age when you get more humor-per-square foot than any other time in a child's life). According to Mother, the traffic was just horrible, with cars darting in and out all trying to get out of the city. Gabe looked over at my mother and offered his best explanation for the chaos. "Gwanny," he drawled in his little Texas accent, "nobody knows where they lee-uve."

I also love the story of the grandmother who was babysitting her young grandchild, a story where the grandmother ended up wondering just who was teaching whom. As they sat coloring pictures the grandmother decided to sneak in a little education. She held up a crayon and asked her granddaughter, "What color is this?" The little girl obediently answered, "It's red." Then the grandmother picked up another color crayon and asked, "Now, can you tell me what this color is?" Again the child answered correctly: "Its blue, Grandma." On and on the little scene played out until finally, in exasperation, the child responded, "Grandma, I really think you should figure out some of these for yourself!"

My friends Taylor and Shalmir Nichols sent a recent report illustrating hilariously just how much of the world's grown-up rhetoric settles between the ears of wee ones. It seems Shalmir's three-year-old granddaughter, Abby, recently entered the world of preschool. A little boy in her class had apparently been giving Abby a hard time. "He even pushed me today," Abby cried to her mother, her tiny arms outstretched in exasperation.

"Oh, my!" her mother empathized. "What did you tell him?"

Abby put hands to hips and in no uncertain terms explained, "I told him to 'Stop the Violence!'" (I wonder if there will be

Wee Little Law School Learning Centers springing up around the country?)

Perhaps you've heard the following pint-sized words of wisdom coming from the brains of babes:

Never ask your three-year-old brother to hold a tomato.

When your mom is mad at your dad, don't let her brush your hair.

Or my personal favorite: Never hold a dust buster and a cat at the same time.

Where would we be without a child to explain the world to us? I'll tell you where we'd be—we'd be without some of the best grin-producing stories in the world of grandparenthood. So next time you are tempted to rush a conversation with a little grandchild, perhaps you might find it worth your time to let him or her bend your ear and provoke a smile worth sharing. (And if you really want to savor the treasure, grab a pen and paper and take notes while your grandchild is expounding. You might have a bestseller on your hands someday!)

□ □ □

When I was a child, I talked like a child, I thought like a child, I reasoned like a child.

1 CORINTHIANS 13:11

13

How to Talk So Grandkids Will Listen

What children expect from grown-ups is not to be "understood," but only to be loved, even though this love may be expressed clumsily or in sternness.

CARL ZUCKER

Zeke, tell me how your architecture classes are coming along. Any new projects?"

"Rachel, what do you think I should do to brighten this room?"

"Gabe, what's the latest, hottest video game that you like?"

"Zach, it's been too long since you've caught me up on yourself. Sit a spell and tell me what's happening."

One of the greatest joys of my life was watching how skillfully my mom and dad could get each of my four very different children to settle in with them for long, meandering, happy sessions of simple conversing. My friend Sandra Aldrich has a saying for her kids and grandkids when she senses they need to talk. "Haul it on in here, Honey," she tells them in her wonderful Kentucky accent and in doing so invites them to bring any burdens and welcomes them into the warmth of her loving embrace.

Now my children are all nearly grown, and still they love few things more than a cup of coffee around the kitchen table at Granny and Daddy George's ranch-style house in their quaint little Texas town. We've dubbed their home "The Ponderosa," and it is certainly a place where all who enter can hang their hats, put their boots up, set a spell, and shoot the breeze with two of the best conversationalists this side of the Rio Grande.

What is my folks' secret to bringing out the "talker" in their grandchildren? Here are some of the tricks of the conversing trade that I've noticed them using:

• *They give my kids their full attention.* They make direct eye contact with their grandkids and screen out as many interruptions as they can. If the conversation is important, they take the phone off the hook or let the answering machine gather all incoming calls for the duration. My father will often put on a soft CD instead of a television. Candlelight or firelight is always cozy and something hot or iced to drink is nice.

Though it is tempting to do busy work as you talk, and there are times for this, kids often feel you are not fully listening if you are knitting or whittling. If you do something with your hands, you might do something rather mindless that both you and your grandchild can enjoy as you talk. Shelling peas on the front porch can keep your hands busy but your mind free to chat.

- *They don't dominate the conversation.* At least half of any conversations with their grandchildren is spent listening and asking good, open-ended, interesting questions. Just because grandparents are adults doesn't mean they try to answer all of the kids' questions or give them the answers, as tempting as that might be.

- *They make themselves available.* When we visited my parents' home, there would be much lingering after breakfast or mealtimes. Clean-up could wait if conversation was going. Refills on coffee, a nice dessert, or adjourning to the living room with hot cups of tea said to my children, "Don't hurry off! Stick around a little longer and let's catch up."

- *Schedule in "do-nothing" time.* Mother purposely kept schedules easy and low key when we came to visit. A jigsaw puzzle was often waiting to be done, and she invited the kids over to talk and work the puzzle at the same time. Mom and Dad also take walks, bake cookies, or do other activities that are unhurried. Sometimes the best talks begin when the body is engaged in something creative or methodical.

- *They ask older grandchildren for their opinions.* As my kids got older my parents asked them their opinions on current issues, politics, and religion. They listen carefully to what their grandchildren have to say and question them about the consequences of what they say so they learn to process thoughts from start to finish. My father and mother are both well-read and truly curious about what my children think on the deeper issues of life. The key is that they listen without judgment (which isn't always easy!).

- *They ask their grandchildren to teach them something.* Another way my parents reached out was by requesting assistance with jobs to make their grandchildren feel useful and grownup. Mom and Dad have taught them plenty of things, so they're giving them a chance to return the favor. Kids can read a map, rearrange a cupboard, plant a flower bed, or help with computers. And my parents always thank them for their help. Kids, like adults, enjoy the feeling of being needed.

• *My mother is also liberal with love pats on the hands and shoulders of her grandchildren.* This, coupled with eye contact and good follow-up questions to my children's comments, makes them feel enormously valued at grandma's kitchen table.

With a plate of homemade (or store-bought) oatmeal cookies and cup of coffee or cold glass of milk, it's no wonder my children still love to visit their grandparents! There's love in Mom and Dad's listening, tenderness in their talking, and plenty of laughter to keep the grandkids coming back for more.

*Wherefore, my beloved brethren, let every man
be swift to hear, slow to speak, slow to wrath.*

JAMES 1:19 KJV

14

One Ringy-Dingy

I just called to say, "I love you," I just
called to say how much I care...
STEVIE WONDER

One of the most fun parts of grandparenting is the first time a grandson or granddaughter utters a shy little "Hi, Grandma" into the telephone. Normally mature and sane women have been known to drop the phone and squeal, "My grandchild just said 'Hi, Bammaw!' to anyone within earshot. It's a huge milestone in Grandparentville because once you can get a toddler to enjoy talking on the phone, that precious little voice is only a few rings away.

Susan M. Kettmann, author of *The 12 Rules of Grandparenting: A New Look at Traditional Roles and How to Break Them,* makes these suggestions for getting the most out of Ma Bell or Nextel.

- *Make calls regular and predictable.* To help children become more comfortable talking with you, make your phone calls regular and expected. Setting aside a regular time to spend with each grandchild on the telephone tells them they are special and reminds them that they are on your mind. It also enables them to organize things they want to say, particularly in reference to past conversations.

- *Mail items you can talk about.* To encourage better conversations with grandchildren who live far away, it can help to send a photograph of yourself to put by the telephone so they can associate it with your voice. You can also mail newspaper clippings, travel brochures, and photographs to discuss at a later date when there are lulls in the conversation. You might give them a "Telephone Folder," decorated with their name, to be kept next to the phone so everything is handy.

- *Try daydreaming together.* If you run out of things to talk about, try daydreaming together. Even better, make daydreaming a regular part of your telephone conversations. Begin by saying something like "I wish we were together today. Where could we go and what would we see?" The possibilities with such open-ended play are endless. And best of all, you send a message that you care about what she or he is thinking!

- *Share stories about your childhood.* Your grandchildren will love it if you share stories about things that happened to you when you were their age. They will also enjoy hearing about what their parents were like when they were children. You can draw closer while passing on family history.

Not only are there telephones, but now we can email our offspring's offspring! My parents have found this an enormous boon and time-saving way to keep up with their teenage grandkids who are so hard to pin down. Teens love getting email and often express themselves more deeply and fully in the written word than they can with words. Recently my son Gabe, at age 16, decided he had some thoughts worth expressing so he began to write "Gabe's deep thought of the day" to family and friends at school. We all encouraged him so much that before long he was reading his "deep thought" of the day as part of his school's morning intercom messages. Now he is gathering them for a book he wants to write someday. Perhaps you computer savvy grandmas could exchange a "deep thought of the week" with your grandchild and save them into a file that someday you can turn into a homemade book.

Whatever form of communication you choose doesn't really matter—just find a creative way to reach out and touch someone you love—someone who calls you by one of the most wonderful names in the world, be it Grandma, Granny, Mee-Ma, Nonnie, Nana, Nonna, or Bammaw.

Let your conversation be always full of grace, seasoned with salt, so that you may know how to answer everyone.
COLOSSIANS 4:6

15

Five-Minute Fun

I have a warm feeling after playing with my
grandchildren. It's the liniment working.
AUTHOR UNKNOWN

With a few items you have around the house (including what is left of the creative right side of your brain), it only takes five minutes to perk the interest of a bored grandchild. My cousin Jamie and I have wonderful memories of making little box houses out of sacks and scraps of material at our grandmother's house for our Troll dolls or Little Kiddles, which were so popular in the late sixties. All we needed were scissors, free access to Nonnie's raw materials (her craft drawer and box of material scraps), safety pins (to secure the cut-out, hemless dresses), and a big imagination. Nonnie also had to tolerate—and maybe even welcomed—a little mess in order to nurture our creativity. (Okay, perhaps a LOT of mess. Nonnie is no longer here on this earth, but this memory still lingers in my 47-year-old mind.)

Is your idea well running a little dry? Here are some quick ideas for a morning or afternoon full of "grandma 'n' me" fun to prime your creativity pump.

- *Paper Caper:* A stack of colorful paper and a library (or purchased) book on paper airplanes or origami can keep a kid occupied all afternoon.

- *Create an instant water orchestra:* Line four or more empty glasses in a row on the kitchen table. Pour water into each glass; the first glass will have only an inch of water, then vary the amounts for the remaining glasses until the last glass is almost completely full. Add a drop or two of food coloring into each glass. Now gently tap each glass with the spoon. Each makes a different sound!

- *Create rainbow fish together.* Cut a pie-shaped wedge out of a cheap paper plate. (This will be the fish's tail.) Glue the pointed tip of the tail to the opposite, uncut end of the paper plate. Tear off pieces of colored tissue paper and glue them to the body and tail. For a more textured look, crumple the pieces of tissue paper before gluing them onto the plate.

- *Another fun fishy activity* for little tots who aren't quite old enough for fishing with grandpa yet is to cut out several simple paper fish shapes—about 4" by 3". Put a paper clip on each fish, and lay them on your carpet "pond." Attach a magnet to a string and tie the end of the string to any sort of stick to make a "fishing pole." Then let your little grandchildren go fishing—attracting the paper fish with the magnet—to their heart's delight. If they are old enough to color or paint, let them decorate their "fishies."

- *Ever heard of painted toast?* Guaranteed to wow any kid at the breakfast table! Pour a small amount of milk into a few drinking cups. Add a few drops of food coloring to each cup (a different color for each). Using a paintbrush, paint designs or pictures onto the bread. Don't soak the bread—use just enough paint for the picture to show up. Now toast the bread for edible art! Voila! Breakfast with grandma is now a work of art.

Borrow or invest in a good, easy craft book to stimulate the ole imagination in both yourself and your grandchildren, who will love leafing through colorful idea books of things to do. True, your kitchen or living room may be a mess once they are finished with their afternoon of originality, but you'll leave your grandkids with colorful memories of old-fashioned, homemade love. And what is more important—a clean house or full hearts?

□ □ □

An empty stable stays clean—but there
is no income from an empty stable.

PROVERB 14:4 TLB

16

Step by Step-Grandparent

*Family means putting your arms around
each other and being there.*

BARBARA BUSH

Two of my dearest friends inherited "instant grandchildren" when their sons married women who had children. Though my friends didn't have the advantage of being at their step-grandchildren's births or watching them learn to walk and talk, they determined to love and become the best grandparents they could be to the little lives God brought to their doors. It's been a joy for me to observe the transition from the "getting to know you" stage to "coming to love you" place in grandparenting children from a previous marriage.

Approximately 60 percent of remarriages involve an adult

with physical custody of one or more children. It only stands to reason that up to 33 percent of persons 65 years and older are step-grandparents. Leading researchers in the field of grand-parenting have listed "age at which the step-grandchild enters the family" as a key factor in determining the strength of the relationship between step-grandparent and step-grandchild. The younger the child enters the family, the stronger and more positive the relationship develops over time.

But many step-grandchildren are introduced into the family at a later age. Then everyone is a stranger. You don't know them; they don't know you or the thousands of little nuances that create a loving relationship. Research suggests that older children experience more difficulty adjusting in step-families.

So how do you learn to love a new stepchild? What if this child is older or resistant to your love? Here are some suggestions gleaned from a few step-grandma pros.

Time

Make a point of spending quality, one-on-one time with this new member of your family. Talk to him (or her), ask questions, listen, watch, take an avid interest. Go beyond your limits and stretch. Find out who he is and what makes him tick. Give him a chance to know who you are and figure out his place in your life. How? There's no substitute for t-i-m-e. This takes thoughtfulness and planning ahead. Does the child love baseball? Get some tickets for both of you to see his favorite sport's team play. Do you see her eyeing the piano when she comes to visit? Ask if she might like you to teach her an easy song. Is she a teenager in love with the mall and glamor? Take her with you to get a free makeover or get some glamor shots made just for fun. The trick is to study your grandchild's interests, and then think of an activity that would allow you to enjoy a little one-on-one time in an area he is already familiar with.

All Things Being Equal

There should be no difference in your actions when dealing with natural and step-grandchildren, even though your feelings may take awhile to line up with how you treat the new additions to your family. Of course, you have to take into consideration personal taste and personality. All kids are different, unique individuals. Don't give her a doll for Christmas if you know she prefers a new shirt just because your other grandchild is getting a doll. But don't give her a doll if your "real" grandchild is getting a new bedroom suite. (I know this example sounds outrageous but the stories from "step-grands" of being treated like an afterthought are myriad and some of them outrageous in the favoritism.) When talking to the kids, don't focus all your attention, all your praise, on one and not the other. Every effort has to be made not to make your step-grandchild feel like a lesser person than the natural grandchild.

Create New Traditions

Gene and Carol Kent became instant step-grandparents to two adorable little girls, Chelsea and Hannah, several years ago. To create instant bonding, the girls began calling Gene and Carol "Grampy" and "Grammy" right away. The girls were young, which made it easier. Just as soon as possible, if the step-grands will accept the idea, give them permission to call you a "grand-parenty" name they like. Gene started a tradition of taking the girls for a "Grampy and Me" breakfast date every time they come into town. The girls love puppets and Carol, who used to teach speech and drama before becoming a national author and speaker, was an instant, willing, and enthusiastic audience to her step-granddaughters' performances. The girls look forward to creating new "shows" to share with Grammy. This quickly became a family tradition that bonded and nurtured the lives of everyone in this new blended situation. When I visited Chelsea and Hannah, I got to be an honorary "Aunt Becky" and was treated like family at these living-room puppet shows.

One of the best ways to bond with children is to pray for them. Stormie Omartian's book *The Power of a Praying Parent* is just as powerful for grandparents or step-grandparents wanting to connect with children and see them grow spiritually and emotionally healthy. How many stories have we heard about a "grandma who prayed for me"—and brought a rebellious young man or woman home to the hearth of God?

Perhaps the number one way to reach a new step-grandchild (or any child), after all, is on our knees.

□ □ □

And this is my prayer: that your love
may abound more and more.

PHILIPPIANS 1:9

17

Sunday School Lessons

I know why families were created with all their imperfections. They humanize you.

ANAÏS NIN

Behind the scenes of every grandmother who has lovingly taken her young grandson or granddaughter to church, there is a story to make the angels chuckle. Recently I received an email chockful of just such anecdotes. I dare you not to grin at these spiritual nuggets of truth, from the mouths of church-attending grandbabes:

Three-year-old Reese: "Our Father, Who does art in heaven, Harold is His name. Amen."

A little boy was overheard praying: "Lord, if you can't

71

make me a better boy, don't worry about it. I'm having a real good time like I am."

• A Sunday school class was studying the Ten Commandments. They were ready to discuss the last one. The teacher asked if anyone could tell her what it was. Susie raised her hand, stood tall, and quoted, "Thou shall not take the covers off the neighbor's wife."

• After church little Jason sobbed all the way home in the backseat of the car. His father asked him three times what was wrong. Finally the boy replied, "That preacher said he wanted us brought up in a Christian home, and I wanted to stay with you guys."

• I had been teaching my three-year-old daughter, Caitlin, the Lord's Prayer for several evenings at bedtime. She would repeat the lines of the prayer after me. Finally she decided to go solo. I listened with pride as she carefully enunciated each word right up to the end of the prayer. "Lead us not into temptation," she prayed, "but deliver us some email. Amen."

• A Sunday school teacher asked her children as they were on the way to church service, "And why is it necessary to be quiet in church?" One bright girl replied, "Because people are sleeping."

• Six-year-old Angie and her four-year-old brother, Joel, were sitting together in church. Joel giggled, sang, and talked out loud. Finally his big sister had enough. "You're not supposed to talk out loud in church."

"Why? Who's going to stop me?" Joel asked.

Angie pointed to the back of the church and said, "See those two men standing by the door? They're hushers."

A mother was preparing pancakes for her sons, Kevin, 5, and Ryan, 3. The boys began to argue over who would get the first pancake. Their mother saw the opportunity for a moral lesson. "If Jesus were sitting here, He would say, "Let my brother have the first pancake. I can wait." Kevin turned to his younger brother and said, "Ryan, you play the part of Jesus!"

A father was at the beach with his children when his four-year-old son ran up to him, grabbed his hand, and led him to the shore where a seagull lay dead in the sand. "Daddy, what happened to him?" the boy asked. "He died and went to heaven," the dad replied. The little boy, eyes wide, asked, "Did God throw him back down?"

A wife invited some people to dinner. At the table she turned to their six-year-old daughter and asked, "Would you like to say the blessing?"

"I wouldn't know what to say," replied the girl.

"Just say what you hear Mommy say," replied the woman.

The girl bowed her head and said, "Lord, why on earth did I invite all these people for dinner?"

□ □ □

May the LORD bless you from Zion all the days of your life...and may you live to see your children's children.

PSALM 128:5-6

18

"Read Me a Book, Grandma!"

Now, listen, Frankie, it's going to be a long cold winter and I baby-sit in the evenings AND I NEED READING MATTER, NOW. DON'T START SITTING AROUND, GO FIND ME SOME BOOKS.

HANNAH HANFF, CORRESPONDENCE WITH A BOOKSHOP OWNER IN
84 CHARING CROSS ROAD

I love children's books and have a stash of my favorite illustrated books tucked away in a cedar chest awaiting the appearance of grandchildren in my life. My children's paternal grandmother, Beverly, bought a little "Golden Book" about once a month as her children were growing up, and so when the grandchildren arrived she had a huge drawer full of books for the kids to read. Her eight grandchildren loved them!

If you live near your grandchildren, you might consider a "Going to the Library with Grandma" day about once every two weeks. Perhaps you could pick them up in the late morning (libraries often have programs for kids at this time), and then you can treat them to a burger lunch at their favorite fast-food restaurant (with a playland). After eating, take them to your house for a little "read-aloud 'n' snuggle" under a big quilt right before their naptime. In fact, you might dub a unique blanket or quilt "Grandma's Reading Quilt" as a special accessory to your reading times together.

There are wonderful chapter books available for early readers, but a universal favorite among kids of all ages is picture books. (And some picture books are so beautifully illustrated, they make wonderful "art appreciation" experiences.) Even a nine- or ten-year-old will enjoy reading along with their younger siblings if you choose a lively illustrated book to read. We never really outgrow a love for pictures on pages!

Here's a treasure trove of grandparent-friendly read-alouds to get you started. All you need is this list, a library card, and a willing child—and you have yourself a ready-made, read-aloud gold mine guaranteed to nurture loving relationships between you and your grandchildren. I have many of these books in my personal collection and read most of them to eager first-graders when I was a public schoolteacher.

Two Must-Have Reading Resources

Hunt, Gladys. *Honey for a Child's Heart.* Zondervan, 2002.

First released in the early sixties, this classic resource book has been recently updated. Hunt has compiled a valuable list of the best books, old and new, that elevate family values and stem from a Christian worldview.

Trelease, Jim. *The Read-Aloud Handbook*. Sixth ed.: Penguin, 2006.

Like *Honey for a Child's Heart,* this book has a fabulous annotated book list. His book *Hey! Listen to This: Stories to Read-Aloud* (Penguin, 1992) serves as a reading "sampler" with excerpts of some great read-aloud stories from classic books. His introduction about the importance of reading aloud to children will inspire you to take time out for books with your grandkids.

Here are some of my favorite books for children.

Early Reading...

Kunhardt, Edith. *Pat the Puppy.* Golden Books, 2001.

A wonderful first book to read to your grandbaby. Like the more famous classic *Pat the Bunny,* this book has lots of fun things to do, but with the added bonus of being about grandparents. Your wee one can fasten Grandma's Velcro jogging shoes or feel her shiny sunglasses. Too fun!

Hodges, Lynn and Sue Buchanan. *I Love You This Much.* ZonderKidz, 2001. John Bendall Brunello, illus.

I heard this book read and sung by the authors, live and in person (in a friend's living room) and bought three copies right away. The book is irresistibly written and illustrated, plus the CD of the lullaby has an easy, singable melody that you'll find yourself humming in no time. I gave one to each of my kids—and they were all over age 16 at the time! Check out any book by Sue and Lynn. You'll not be disappointed.

Martin, Bill, and John Archambault, *Barn Dance!* Henry Holt & Co., 1988. Ted Rand, illus.

I practically wore this book out when I was a first-grade teacher. I dare you to try to read it aloud without tapping your toes or wanting to kick up your heels. Pure joy to read aloud again and again. (Read aloud hint: Start out very softly, get louder as the barn comes alive with its critter hoe-down and then lower your voice as the book nears its sleepy end.) This great book beautifully captures the excitement of an old-fashioned barn dance. If you enjoy reading books with a southern style, toe-tapping patter, also check out *Possum Come A-Knockin'* by Nancy Van Laan (Dragonfly Books, 1992).

A fun aside: I once took my daughter, Rachel, to a book signing by beloved children's author Bill Martin, when she was in the first grade. He was so kind; he reminded me of a friendly giant. She was star-struck, having read so many of his classic first readers. Don't miss his books *Brown Bear, Brown Bear, What Do You See?* and *Chicka-Chicka Boom Boom.* Your grandkids will be reading right along with you on the second read-through. (Or third, fourth, or one hundredth.)

Munsch, Robert. *Love You Forever.* Firefly Books Ltd., 1986. Sheila McGraw, illus.

If you can read through this book without getting a tear in your eye and a lump in your throat you are a stronger woman than I am. My first graders loved to get me to read this book because they knew I'd always get choked up at the ending!

Rylant, Cynthia. *When I Was Young in the Mountains.* Puffin, 1993. Illustrated by Diane Goode.

One of my favorite picture books about a little girl growing up in the mountains with her grandparents. It's a Caldecott Honor Book, and it will transport you and your grandchild to another time and place.

Silverstein, Shel. *Where the Sidewalk Ends.* 30th Anniversary ed.: HarperCollins, 2004.

The perfect laugh-aloud and read-aloud collection of poems. If you start them out on this, your grand-children will not yawn when you suggest reading poetry together.

Wood, Audry. *The Napping House.* Red Wagon Books, 2000. Don Wood, illus.

Perfect for preschool insomniacs! A whimsically illustrated and rhythmic, repetitive, bedtime story. Especially fun for grandmas as the book showcases a "snoring granny, a dreaming child, a dozing dog" and so on. And the whole sleepy household congregates on Granny's bed!

Chapter Book Reading

Below are some favorite read-aloud "chapter book" classics that never grow old. If you are good at skipping the boring parts and reading ahead to the action and dialogue, you can begin reading short chapter books when your children are as young as five. They'll love having a continuous story to look forward to reading each night.

Dahl, Roald. *James and the Giant Peach.* Puffin, 2000. Lane Smith, illus.

> Best known for his book (and the movie) *Charlie and the Chocolate Factory,* Roald Dahl's sometimes dark, but creatively funny books are a joy to read aloud—especially this one because there are so many hilarious and atrocious characters. If you specialize in hamming it up and doing "voices," you'll have a ball with this book. I read this one to my children on a long car trip, and they never grew tired of it. My sons especially got hooked on Dahl's books.

Freeman, Becky. *Camp Wanna Banana Mysteries.* Waterbrook Press.

> Several years ago, I wrote this series of easy reading, fast-paced, funny mysteries for ages 7 through 11. They were wonderfully received by moms, kids, and teachers—but short-lived in print due to some changes within the publishing company. You can find used copies, however, on Amazon and other sources, if you are interested in ordering them. And some local church and public libraries carry them. I hope to get them back in print someday, as there is a real shortage of easy, page-turning chapter books for children. I tried to write these books with only the "good parts" in mind. No long, boring passages!

Wild Rattle in the Woods
Secrets of Thief Cave
Peanut Butter Burglary
Yellow Eyes in the Dark
Riddles from the Hope Chest

Wallace, Bill. *Beauty.* Aladdin, 1990.

My second-born son was enamored of this book about a boy and his beloved horse. Zeke went on to read everything Bill Wallace wrote. In fact, he wrote Bill a letter and Bill wrote such a wonderfully kind response, that Bill, Zeke, and I struck up a bit of a friendship. When it came time to test my first manuscript with readers, Bill was one of the first authors to lend encouragement.

Warner, Gertrude Chandler. *The Boxcar Children.* Albert Whitman & Co., 1989. L. Kate Deal, illus.

This story of runaway siblings who have to make it on their own and end up nesting in an abandoned boxcar has fascinated children for 60 years.

Wilder, Laura Ingalls. *Little House in the Big Woods.* Harper Trophy reprint, 2004. Garth Williams, illus.

This is my favorite "starter-book" in the Ingalls Wilder series. I have warm memories of my teacher reading a chapter a day aloud when I was in third grade. I read "the good parts" to my children when they were four and five.

Bedtime Stories on CD

Here are some ideas for when you're too pooped to read!

Psalty Sleepytime Helpers (www.psalty.com).

> My children adored going to bed with "Psalty" and especially loved this set. My kids are all over age 20 today, and each one can still sing the "sleepytime" song. I'm sure they'll be singing it to their children, and I plan on ordering fresh sets for my grandchildren.

Adventures in Odyssey (www.whitsend.org).

> My stepsons adored these audio CDs as little boys. In fact, Troy, who just graduated from college, asked for a set of them for Christmas this year. He still loves to listen to them at night before drifting off to a peaceful sleep.

Other Quick Mentions

> *The Lion, the Witch, and the Wardrobe*
> *Pilgrim's Progress (simplified version)*
> *The Wind in the Willows*
> *A Wrinkle in Time*

In writing this book, I stumbled on a great website: www.grandloving.com. The authors have a great list of annotated books just about grandparents and grandchildren that you may want to check out and read to your little ones.

Even as I close this chapter I'm thinking of so many wonderful books I've not listed. But this will get you started on your own grandparenting reading adventure. Once you start down the road to reading and get hooked, it's truly a lifelong, never-ending delight. What a gift to share with your grandchildren! Reading is one of life's most portable and affordable diversions. All you need to transport yourself from boredom to adventure is one small library card. Talk about one of the world's greatest bargains!

Happy snuggling, reading, learning, and bonding to you and yours.

□ □ □

[Jesus] went into the synagogue, as was his custom. And he stood up to read.

LUKE 4:16

19

The Art of Growing Young

Winter is on my head, but eternal spring is in my heart.
VICTOR HUGO

I met a kid one day at a local folk festival. He was having an absolute ball playing around with a couple of sticks in front of anybody who would pause long enough to watch the show. I asked this kid, "How old are you anyway?"

"I turned 70 this year," he answered with a grin.

This gentleman was one of several lively senior citizens I met that day. They didn't appear to be ready for retirement homes, although several seemed likely candidates for kindergarten—especially a kindergarten that allowed for plenty of play time. It was the first time in 20 years I found myself thinking, *I can't wait till I get older!*

The stick kid's real name turned out to be Donald De Camp, but he goes by the name "Mr. Bones." This was evident because the word "Bones" was engraved on the back of his leather belt. (Leather belts substitute for business cards and billboards among folk festival types.) He goes by "Mr. Bones" because he plays the bones. Not the ones attached to his skeleton, but two pieces of birds-eye maple carved into the shape and size of a couple of thick bookmarks.

Held loosely between the fingers, the blocks of wood snap out infinite and complicated rhythms to the harmonies of guitars, banjos, dulcimers, and such. Mr. Bones played his sticks two sets at a time—a pair going in each hand. I must say it was an awe-inspiring sight for all who watched this performer at work.

I took advantage of an opportunity to visit with Bones during a break. As the old gentleman wiped the sweat from his forehead, he said, "Man, oh man. I *love* that rhythm!" Now he wasn't referring to a particular rhythm in a particular song. He loved the big idea of rhythm, the entire *concept* of rhythm, any regular beat that allowed him the chance to get out his sticks and play.

He told me that years ago the "bones" were originally made from animal bones, and he'd even found some evidence that "the bones," as musical instruments, had been in existence some 1500 years before Christ. Young Donald picked them up as a child for the pure fun of it and has been playing them for all they're worth ever since.

That's all the information we could squeeze in our conversation because the band started back up again and all his friends began begging him to come out and play with them some more.

He bowed his apologies to us young'uns, shuffled to center stage, closed his eyes for a moment, then went to tapping and dancing and playing those bones. He was wild joy on the loose.

The small crowd followed Bone's every movement and I too stood entranced. I've always been an admirer of old codgers, especially the sort with plenty of twinkles left in their eyes.

I imagine if I were to write a male version of the famous poem, "When I am Old I Shall Wear Purple," it might go something like this:

> When I am old, I shall wear my hair in tufts of sweepy
>   silver 'round the perimeter of my head.
> I shall wear old boots and faded jeans and a tanned
>   leather belt with my name on the back.
> I shall own a crisp white shirt, a black string tie, a hand-
>   some vest and a pocket watch with a gold chain that
>   loops in front.
> I shall close my eyes when I hear the band start up, and
>   I shall wander toward the sounds until the beat col-
>   lides with the joy in my heart.
> And I shall dance.
> Alone, or with a pretty gal, or with my best set of bones.
> And I shall make all the young ones wish they were old—
>   Old enough to shuffle center stage and play
>   with the abandon of an uninhibited soul.

I walked away from that crisp fall evening at the festival feeling somehow younger, almost reborn, for having been in the presence of a seasoned elder who had mastered the fine art of staying childlike at heart.

They will still bear fruit in old age,
they will stay fresh and green.

PSALM 92:14

Когда я состарюсь ~~может~~
~~быть~~ волосы мои станут серебряно
белыми от седин, и на лице
ярко будут впряжены те эмоции
которых было больше за жизнь,
руки выдадут те труды которыми
я трудилась, одежду найду комфор-
ную и обувь, но если Ты заглянешь
мне в глаза Ты увидишь всё
ту же любовь к Тебе - Мой Бог!; и
только заговоришь ко мне, я
с радостью запою тебе хвалу и
мое сердце будет биться в Твоим
ритме и то, что скажешь Ты -
сделаю, куда Поведёшь пойду;
потому что люблю Тебя!
88 И ~~Ты~~ освежишь меня и силы
дашь.

A Grandson's Returning

*What children need most are the essentials
that grandparents provide in abundance.
They give unconditional love, kindness,
patience, humor, comfort, lessons in life.
And, most importantly, cookies.*

RUDOLPH GIULIANI

One of my sons, though heart-wrenchingly lovable at times, has pretty much always been what I call a bit of a "challenge child." In other words, he has kept me on my toes and on my knees a lot. The good news is that he is now 25 and though he still has some struggles, his life is much more stable and happy than it has been in a decade. He's climbed out of more valleys to find new mountaintops than I ever dreamed possible.

Zach has a four-year-old son, whom he adores, named Ethan. Sadly, he and the child's mother didn't stay together long after Ethan was conceived. But Zach loved his every-other weekend visits with his son. My son changed Ethan's diapers, rocked him to sleep, and generally was a great father for the small amounts of time he was able to be with his son. As Ethan grew, Zach taught him to hit a baseball and how to catch a fish. He read him stories, took him for walks, put him down for naps. They were adorable together.

During this time, my precious parents offered to let Zach live with them so he could get on his emotional and financial feet. For a year, Zach was treated to nonstop TLC. My mother made him home-cooked meals, washed his clothes, and gave him unending hugs as only a doting grandmother can do. My father took time to mentor Zach in business, help him get on top of his finances, and gave other practical help. Dad also took him out to play relaxing rounds of golf or to wet a line in the lake in front of my parents' home. Zach joined his grandparents on many of their "old folk" excursions to barbecues, banquets, and parties put on by their "golden years" Sunday school class. Mom and Dad gave every drop of love they had to give into my son's life. Though there were a few rough patches now and again, most often my Dad would say, with a catch in his voice, "Becky, I love that boy like my own son. It has been a gift to have him here, to get this privilege of knowing my grandson so well and feeling so close to him."

Because my own life was in crisis during that time, I was enormously relieved to know my son was in loving, peaceful, and supportive hands.

Last year, Zach decided he needed to make a lot of money in a short amount of time to catch up with his obligations. He announced he was going to Alaska to become a salmon fisherman. It sounded like a wild, fantastical dream—something guys say around campfires when they're feeling macho and adventurous but never do.

To our shock and surprise, Zachary did it. He drove all the way from Texas, stopping in Denver to visit us, and eventually made his way to Seattle. When he called from the boat, I could hear the ocean waves and sea gull sounds in the background. His voice sounded strong and sure and happy.

"Mom," he said, "it's the hardest work I've ever done, but I love it. It's beautiful here, and fishing makes me want to be a better man! Also I've landed on the boat of probably the only fishing captain in Seattle who is a Bible-reading Christian and who doesn't allow alcohol or drugs on the ship. I guess you, Granny, and Grandpa must have been praying."

Every time I talked to Zach as his boat pulled up to port, he sounded better and better. When he got off the boat, a nice paycheck in hand, he and I met in Texas for a visit with Ethan who was three and a half years old. He's sweet and shy and loving, adorable and affectionate. How I ache to be able to be more in this grandson's life. I pray that God will continue to open doors and hearts so this might happen.

Today Zach lives near us in Colorado, and he is currently dating a wonderful gal. He's got a good job and is going to our church. He's making good friends and is torn between the decision to go back out to sea when the salmon are running or to stay here.

Zach has made amazing progress in his life, and I'm proud of him. I'm grateful for every two steps forward, and I try to relax when there's a small step backward now and again by keeping the bigger picture in mind. Progress, not perfection, is the goal. I'm also indebted to my parents, Zach's grandparents, who pray for him daily, who mentored him, and who gave him refuge, respite, and encouragement for a year in their home. I'm also thankful for all of their Sunday school friends who prayed for and loved Zach and asked him to go fishing, play a round of golf, or stop by for some cookies.

The other day Zach was thinking aloud about some of the pressures he's carrying, but also I could hear pride around the edges of his voice as he was taking responsibility for his own life, becoming the man he's wanted to be, the sort of father that Ethan is proud to call Dad.

"No one really understands how hard it has been, and how far I've come," he started to say.

"No one?" I asked with a smile. Zach sometimes forgets all the love around him—that he's never been alone, that his family has been there through all his pain, and they applauded all his gain. Usually a little reminder is all it takes.

"Well," he mused, "that's probably not true. I think my Grandpa does." He took a sip of his coffee, set it down, and smiled. "Yeah, Grandpa probably understands."

To be understood and cared for by another human soul is love in work clothes. It's love that looks beyond our faults and sees our deeper need. It's the unconditional, never-failing, always believing love of God.

And it's also the love of very special grandparents, like Zach's... and probably like you.

Love bears all things, believes all things, hopes all things, endures all things. Love never fails.

1 CORINTHIANS 13:7-8

21

Surprise Acts

When a child is born, so are grandmothers.
JUDITH LEVY

A native-born, lifelong Texan, I never dreamed I'd live any-where but the Lone Star State. But then there are lots of things I never dreamed would happen to me.

I remember being in my late twenties, sitting around the kitchen table at my grandmother's house, up to my earlobes in babies and toddlers, having given birth to four children in less than seven years. I wondered aloud if I'd ever get out of this era of endless diapers before I was the one who would be wearing Depends. It was hard not to feel as though my body had been invaded and rented out to miniature boarders: For a decade little ones were either occupying my uterus, sitting on my lap, getting nourishment from my breasts, or hanging onto my neck while I balanced them on my hip. I had turned into a human feeding/climbing gym.

"I remember those years," said my grandmother Nonnie, who'd birthed seven children in a decade back when she had her babies at home. Home births then weren't because it was the "in and natural thing to do," but because they couldn't afford a doctor or hospital during the Great Depression. "I was perpetually holding a baby. When I finally got everyone else fed and sat down to eat my quickly cooling supper, I'd reach for my food over the top of one of my children's heads. I think I've eaten enough hair off the top of my kids' heads to stuff a mattress."

Aunt Etta laughed and said, "Becky, you know, when I was your age I used to wonder if I'd ever get out of the raising babies stage. But trust me, life is actually pretty long. Just when you think one stage will last forever, that 'act' ends and another one opens up. In some ways, I feel I've lived about ten different lives!"

With the big "5-0" looming before me in just a few years, I have to say my Aunt Etta was right. Since that day in Nonnie's kitchen, I've experienced four major acts in the play of my life. Eventually, my babies grew up into self-feeding, potty-trained children. The curtain closed on Act 1. Then came Act 2. While my children were all in preschool or elementary school, I packed up my own backpack and sack lunch and headed back to college to finish my degree on a part-time basis. When I graduated in 1991 with a degree in Early Childhood Education, I walked across the stage to accept my diploma to the applause of my four children sitting in the front row who ranged from ages 6 through 13. When I discovered that teaching real human first-graders in small quarters for days on end wasn't nearly as much fun as studying about it in college, I became a retired teacher after nine months of faithful service.

The Era of Finishing My Education ended with the acceptance of my first book proposal, coauthored with my mom: *Worms in My Tea & Other Mixed Blessings.* Enter Act 3. Two dozen books and ten years of speaking engagements, along with multiple kids' sports events, carpooling, and senior proms, I found myself suddenly (and shockingly) single, with a newly emptied nest and a big question mark where my preplanned future once stood so firmly in my mind's eye.

Let's just fast-forward past the intermission of Heartache, Despair, Loneliness, and Depression to Act 4, shall we?

The current scene of my life opens in the mountains of Denver, Colorado, where I live, work, love, and flirt with the love of my mid-life years, my husband, Greg. Three of my grown kids have moved to be near us (and the call of the mountains) over the last several months. (We're still working on my daughter, who is taking a bit longer to catch the vision of moving near her mother. The problem is that she's fallen in love with a Texas boy, and I mean the died-in-the-wool kind. He's a slow-talking, "Yes, ma'aming," boots and jeans-wearing country boy, and a rabid Longhorn fan. To uproot him from Texas is going to take an act of God. It's a good thing I believe that a mama's prayer is the shortest route to getting an act of God up and running!)

The first of my children to make the Texas break and move here were Zeke and his wife, Amy. They'd just moved from Dallas to San Antonio where Zeke took a great job working for a well-respected architectural firm. The situation seemed ideal for them. San Antonio and its famous river walk, lively Hispanic culture, great food, and scenic charm were right up their artistic alley.

(Amy is a multitalented freelance artist.) There were also lots of nearby opportunities for Zeke and Amy to enjoy the outdoor sports they loved: rock-climbing, kayaking, rafting, mountain biking. It was a life they'd dreamed of. They were blissful.

Until July came with its not-so-charming 105-degree days pelting down on Zeke and Amy's not-very-insulated rented cottage equipped with one overwrought, antiquated air conditioner. They were in meltdown.

Amy flew up from Texas to Denver during that time to attend a conference and visit with us. She boarded the plane in the sweltering San Antone sun, and then, as if by magic, stepped off the same plane, two hours later, into a scene worthy of a sonnet or at least a John Denver ballad. A light, cool, mountain breeze blew her beautiful long mane of red curls and the Rockies showed off their majesty against a clear blue sky. Opportunities for work, school, and recreational sports beckoned as well.

"We're so moving here," Amy said at the end of the week. (I tried not to do the mama happy dance in her presence, but I could hardly contain my excitement.)

I knew Amy's wifely powers of persuasion, and sure enough, she pulled it off. Within a month she, Zeke, their two beagles, and their fully loaded U-Haul trailer pulled up in front of our house. While Zeke dove right into the architecture master's program at the University of Colorado and both of them looked for work and a place to live, they stayed with us. A funny thing happened when a child of mine moved under our roof for a time. All of my mothering instincts, put on hold for the last few years, came suddenly and fully to the forefront. It was both nice...and a little bit scary for everyone, I think. One day as Zeke was leaving for college, I called to him as he walked out the door toward his truck: "Wait! You forgot your sack lunch I made for you. And don't forget your coat. And it looks like rain; you might need an umbrella and galoshes. I think Greg has some extras."

"Mom, I love you," he said sweetly, obediently taking the lunch but ignoring the coat and rain gear. After a month of being pampered and "mama-ed" nearly to death, he and Amy were *really* ready to get back to their independent, grownup lives. And though Greg and I missed them, we were happy to get back to our fun, flirtatious, and empty-nesting schedule.

The month after Zeke and Amy moved into their new apartment, I was returning from a trip and they offered to pick me up at the airport. When I saw them as I walked toward the baggage claim area, they looked like two kids who had been up to something—something mischievous, something fun. As it turns out, they had been.

"Mom," Zeke said, his arm around his beaming bride, "we're going to have a baby!"

Tears, jumping, squealing, and hugging followed, though not necessarily in that order. Actually there was no order at all, just a powerful tidal wave of joy and the intense sense that at that very moment I was entering another act in the evolving play that is my life.

I'll never forget one precious moment as we drove along in Zeke's truck, Zeke's happy and pregnant wife at his side, his euphoric mother in the backseat. We came to a red light, and Zeke looked back at me, tears in his eyes. "Mom, I'm going to be a dad!" he exclaimed, his voice breaking with the wonder of the word. Dad. Father.

In a few months Zeke added another wonder-filled word to his vocabulary: son. He would be having a son.

And I will be having a grandson, and his name will be Justin Nathaniel (after Amy's beloved younger brother), but we'll call him Nate...or "God's Gift to Our Family."

And so the curtain rises on Act 5 of my life. And I can hardly stand the anticipation.

"For I know the plans I have for you," declares the Lord, "plans...to give you hope and a future."

Jeremiah 29:11

22

A MeeMaw by Any Other Name Is Still a Grandma

Grandmas are moms with lots of frosting.
AUTHOR UNKNOWN

My daughter-in-love, Amy, had a sonogram in her seventh month, and even though the pictures looked like a badly lit black-and-white home movie from the fifties, one thing was clear to all who saw baby Nathaniel rock-climbing and kayaking inside Amy's womb: He looks exactly like Zeke. No pride, just fact. Even Amy's parents agree. "That boy is a little Zeke, all right."

Next weekend, we'll have Amy's baby shower here at my home. My daughter, Rachel, will be flying in from Texas as well, making this a moment all of my children will celebrate together.

I've turned into a shopping-possessed granny. I've never met a baby clothing store I don't like. My best finds thus far are the cutest forest green, orange, and khaki "outdoors sports" outfits, in three-month-old and six-month-old sizes. I ask you, Could there be anything cuter than a baby boy dressed like Crocodile Dundee? I brake for anything baby-related these days—clothes, furniture, accessories, and especially cute little baby boys. I can't keep from commenting to the boy's parents or grandparents, though they are strangers to me, "I'm getting one of those too, pretty soon."

My mother called the other day and said, "Becky, no matter how excited you are, no matter how great you imagine this day to be, you cannot prepare for the enormity of the love that will hit you full force when you hold Nate for the first time. It's a high like no other I can describe. Very different from having your own baby, which has its own euphoria. You just have to experience it."

I remembered the days and months following my firstborn son's birth. How my mother would so often "happen to be in the neighborhood"—a thinly veiled excuse to drop by for a grandbaby fix.

"He won't be this small for very long!" she'd say, scooping him up like long-lost treasure, staring at him as if he were the first baby ever created...or at least the most amazing, smart, beautiful, and talented baby on earth at that point in time. She determined to squeeze all the goodies out of the adorable first years of Zach's life. She did the same with all the grandchildren to follow, although it wasn't quite as easy to give the newly arriving newborns her undivided focus over the heads of grand-toddlers and grand-preschoolers clamoring for her attention as well.

No doubt there was a special bonding that occurred during the "birthin' baby" years between my mother and me. This emotional super-glue that held us together was the shared maternal love for this child—my son, her grandson. Who else would genuinely share my excitement over my son's first giggle, first word, first poop-in-the-potty? The mutual admiration for new life, fresh from heaven, is one of God's most mysterious and powerful female bonding agents.

A few weeks ago Zeke and Amy and I sat around our kitchen table discussing what my "grandmother" name might be. My mother is "Granny," which I think is cute, but, obviously, it is taken. Amy's mother is a seasoned grandmother of two little granddaughters. Her grandma-name is "Mimi" (which I think is adorable) but again, that name is in use. "Grandma" is way too plain a name for a colorful grandmother like I'm going to be. Then Zeke asked, "Why can't you be called Nonnie?"

"But my grandmother was Nonnie," I protested.

"And so," Amy reasoned, "you could honor her by taking on her name."

The thought never occurred to me. I could be a Nonnie too? I have so many warm memories of my Nonnie. She was "Every Grandma"—complete with cotton-print dress, apron, silver hair up in a French twist. She seemed to live in the kitchen, rising early and staying up late to cook something yummy and nurturing for whatever family was visiting at the time. She had a soft lap and ample bosom, making her a human pillow built for rocking babies to sleep and welcoming grandchildren's hugs. Sweet-tempered, gentle, kind, and loving, she never said a cross word to anyone. I've definitely inherited her ample bosom and her love for children. I also seem to be spending a lot more time in the kitchen as I'm experiencing a homemaking renaissance of sorts. More and more of late I find myself happily cooking up big Sunday dinners or Saturday lunches for our growing and blending family of adult children who drop by. I even wear a retro-style apron. Most days my husband says I'm pretty sweet-tempered, gentle, kind, and loving. (We aren't counting PMS days, are we?)

So maybe I'm not so very unlike my grandmother. Nonnie it is. Nonnie I'll be. Or maybe Nonnie with a twist: Nonnie-B?

Or perhaps our best-laid plans will go up in smoke, and Nate will give me his own name, as often happens when the actual grandchild begins to talk. (How else can we explain names like Doodie, Pooky, and MeeMaw? Only an adorable grandchild could persuade grown women to wear such names with pride.)

Ah me. Nate can call me Esmerelda for all I care, as long as I can hold him close to my heart and sing him to sleep and love him forever and always.

□ □ □

He will take great delight in you, he will quiet you with his love, he will rejoice over you with singing.

Zephaniah 3:17

23

The Original Granddaughter

A child needs a grandparent, anybody's grandparent, to grow a little more securely into an unfamiliar world.

CHARLES AND ANN MORSE

Because I don't think any gift book for grandmothers can possibly be complete without including the wonderful piece written by a child called "What a Grandmother Is," I researched its origins on the internet. To my delight, I found this open letter by Sandra L. DeMattia (formerly Sandra L. Doty). It came as a great surprise that the original piece was more than 53 years old. But I'm jumping ahead. Below is a copy of the open letter, with the "What a Grandmother Is" piece included in its original form.

"What a Grandmother Is"

A grandmother is a lady who has no children of her own, so she likes other people's little girls. A grandfather is a man grandmother. He goes for walks with the boys, and they talk about fishing and tractors and things like that.

Grandmas don't have to do anything except be there. They're old, so they shouldn't play hard or run. It is enough if they drive us to market where the pretend horse is and have lots of dimes ready. Or if they take us for walks, they should slow down past pretty leaves and caterpillars. They should never, ever say "Hurry Up."

Usually they are fat, but not too fat to tie kids' shoes. They wear glasses and funny underwear. They can take off their teeth and gums.

It is better if they don't typewrite or play cards except with us. They don't have to be smart, only answer questions like why dogs hate cats and how come God isn't married. They don't talk baby talk like visitors do, because it is hard to understand. When they read to us they don't skip or mind if it is the same story again.

In her letter to me, Sandra went on to say,

As you may have guessed by now, I am the little girl who said those words 53 years ago.

My first "official speech" has had quite a journey since then. It was "discovered" by Dr. Dobson in the late 70's and then some 25 years later he was informed by Aunt Grace (who had the original copy) that the child in question was not an eight-year-old, but was only about 3½ when she was asked by her grandmother, "What is a Grandmother?"

The quote has appeared in at least two of Dr. James Dobson's books (*What Wives Wish Their Husbands Knew About Women* and *Home with a Heart*) and has been broadcast numerous times on his radio program *Focus on the Family*.

Over the past 53 years the origin and authorship of "What a Grandmother Is" has evolved into somewhat of an urban legend. My thoughts about grandparents obviously struck a chord in the hearts of millions of people and I would wish everyone to continue to make people smile...perhaps for another 53 years.

Sincerely,

Sandra L. DeMattia (formerly Sandra L. Doty)

A few days after rediscovering this charming piece, I was struck with journalistic curiosity. I found Sandra's email and wrote her, asking her if she'd share a bit more about her life.

It turns out that little 3½-year-old Sandra has lived quite the fascinating life and is still as capable of bringing a smile and capturing hearts today as she was so many years ago. Here are portions of her correspondence with me, in her own words.

The fact that you took the time to get back to me is just another "tap on the shoulder" from God to remind me that "The Grandmother" is still "a work in progress." It seems almost prophetic that at that early age I would set down the rules for being a grandparent, only to follow them years later. I have no children of my own...so I "borrow other people's little girls."

To answer a few questions, *"Why did my grandmother take the time to write down my words so long ago?"* By way of background, I was born in 1948 in West Springfield, Massachusetts. I was the youngest of three, and the only girl. We lived adjacent to my grandfather's market garden and wholesale florist business. My grandparents lived just down the street and two of my father's brothers (and families) lived within the same "farm complex."

The office and florist shop were at the hub of this, and throughout the day there was an endless parade of adults and children. As a toddler I just assumed that I had three fathers, three mothers, seven brothers and sisters, and two grandparents.

My grandmother would spend part of her day at the flowershop and would often watch the grandchildren while the parents worked.

I think my grandmother may have been trying to shed some light on the difference between aunts, uncles, and parents when she asked me to explain what a grandmother was. She was a firm believer in the theory that in order for a child to learn you must first determine their "starting point" and only tell them what they ask. Too much information only confuses the issue.

How did the piece end up in Dr. Dobson's possession? My grandmother took notes and sent my answer in a letter to her sister (my Great Aunt Merriam) in San Diego.

Aunt Merriam worked in a doctor's office at the time and must have shared it with someone, who shared it with someone, who shared it with someone until it showed up 20 years later in a newsletter at the Children's Hospital in San Francisco. That is where Dr. James Dobson found it and began using it in his broadcasts and later in two of his books.

What significance does this little grandma/granddaughter dictation mean to my life now, looking back? No matter how perfect their lives or their living of it, everyone will at some point question themselves and their actions. Some will turn to God for the answer, others will seek help from more earthly creatures. Apparently I was lucky enough to have God at my side from the very beginning, guiding me at every turn. He knew that the honest thoughts of a child get clouded over as we mature with the challenges of everyday living...so He "asked" my Grandmother to write down my thoughts "for future reference." He also presented Dr. Dobson (the most prolific author of childrearing books in the 20th century) with a copy to publish and read on his broadcasts. I think God may have even turned on Aunt Grace's radio that day to hear the broadcast and authenticate the authorship and thus complete the circle.

The question of universal appeal is simple. God loves all of his children. Why does it keep reentering my life? Well...unlike opportunity, God has been known to knock often...just in case we aren't paying attention.

And lastly...as to any questions about my childless state.
In my early teens I made a decision not to have children"
because I carried a gene that would most likely be passed
on to my offsprings. I was born with congenital lymph-
edema (Milroy's Disease) of the lower legs. Simply put,
I have enlarged legs from the knee down and retain large
amounts of fluid. I was either born with a defective or
missing valve in my lymph system. My mother was born
with it as was one of her brothers and her mother. Apparently I was the last in that line with it...so I opted to end
the saga. I kept busy in my twenties and thirties with
a career, and at the ripe old age of 39, in 1987, I married (for the first time...and last) a man 342 months my
senior. [Becky's note: Yes, that translates to be 28½ years.
And if that doesn't strike you as interesting, Sandra and
"Mr. Andrew" as she calls her beloved Italian husband
have been married for 18 years.]

Throughout my life I have been the object of stares
from both children and adults. Being "different" is one of
the most difficult job descriptions that God could have
given me. But he also gave me a wonderful family with
a strong faith in Him to help me along. I won't try to
tell you that I never wondered "Why Me?" or "Is there
a cure?" What it has done for me is show me how to
treat my fellow man with respect...no matter what our
differences. How to forgive other people's shortcomings
and to dwell on the positive aspects of everyday life and
in general put the really important things in life in true

prospective. Life (as I know it) has given me a chance to find humor where misery would like to live.

I think that I made the right decision on having "little girls" of my own...because there are so many little girls out there to borrow.

Sandra DeMattia

In 1997, Sandra and "Mr. Andrew" moved from Vermont to South Carolina, where they live today. Sandra, taking after her grandmother, writes vivid slice-of-life stories to her relatives that she calls "Letters from the Lemonade Stand."

So, Grandmas, reread "What a Grandmother Is," and, just for fun, the next time your grandson or granddaughter comes over (or you go to visit), ask him or her to tell you what he thinks a grandmother is. You may be surprised and delighted to discover yourself anew from a child's eye view.

□ □ □

And whoever welcomes this little
child in my name, welcomes me.

LUKE 9:48

From Becky Freeman Johnson...

☐ ☐ ☐

With my new marriage and a nearby (and ever-growing) passel of children-turned-adults, I've taken on lots of happy new roles: wife, mom, mother-in-law, stepmom, and grandmother. I also support my husband, Greg, in his literary business with editing, client support, and hostessing.

Because of these wonderful changes and the time it takes to be available to my family, I rarely do public speaking. However, if you need a good speaker for your event, may I recommend my good friends Gene and Carol Kent at Speak Up Speaker Services? They can be contacted at www.speakupspeakerservices.com.

For updates on my books and other news or information visit me at

www.yellowroseeditorial.com

Becky Freeman Johnson's brand-new series

HeartLite Stories

will bless your heart and tickle your funny bone!

*BECKY'S TRADEMARK HUMOR AND WARMTH SHINE IN HER
HEARTLITE STORIES. EACH ATTRACTIVE, HARDCOVER BOOK
OVERFLOWS WITH STORIES OF JOY AND INSPIRATION.*

It's Fun to Be Your Friend

When lives intersect and a bond between women is formed, the treasures of faithfulness, loyalty, and authenticity are discovered. Becky reflects on all these gifts and more as she shares joy-filled stories about how a cherished friend knows us better than we know ourselves, extends forgiveness and grace, believes in our goodness and gifts, offers silence or conversation when we need it, and becomes a reflection of unconditional love.

It's Fun to Be Your Sister

In this gathering of delightful stories about the connection between sisters and sisters-of-the-heart, each engaging chapter reveals why a sister is the gift that keeps on giving. Women with sisters are able to laugh more at life and at themselves, rest in what they have in common, find blessings and inspiration in each other, walk through life with joy and laughter, and share the biggest trials and the simplest pleasures.

It's Fun to Be a Mom

Becky invites women to take a break, catch their breath, and savor stories of pure joy about the privilege, the labor, and the gift of motherhood. These engaging, short tales lead moms to embrace the habits of highly real moms, the strange miracle of breast feeding, the loss of brain cells when one gains a child, the quest for sleep and romance after kids, and the amazing strength of their own mothers.

It's Fun to Be a Grandma

A grandma is to be revered and celebrated. And Becky does just that with stories from her life as a granddaughter and grandmother. With warmth, insight, and her trademark humor, Becky lifts up these special women who believe wholeheartedly in their children and grandchildren, become the keeper of stories and memories, have incomparable strength of spirit and heart, show the women following them how to live richly, and never tire of talking to or about their grandbabies.